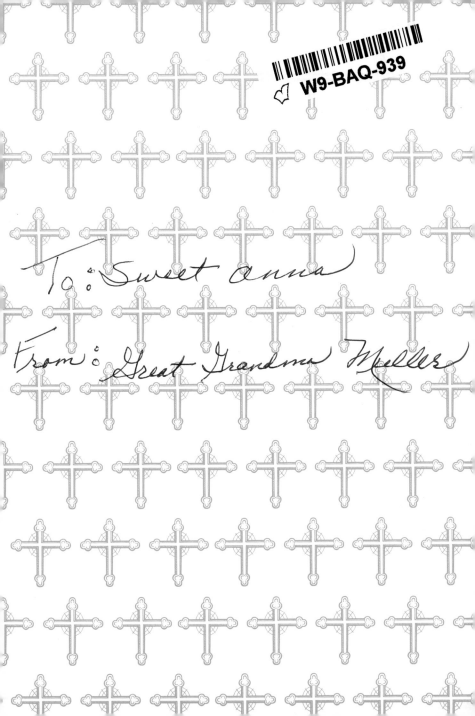

To: Sweet Anna

From: Great Grandma Mueller

Daily Prayers
for Catholic Children

by
Daniel A. Lord, S.J.

Before You Begin To Pray

Before you start to pray, always remember:

That you are God's child. That He is very close to you. He can hear all that you say. He will give you what you ask for, if it is good for you. He loves you very much.

When you pray, you are just talking to God. And God is the One who loves you most. So prayer is easy. It is just talking things over with God. God is waiting to hear you when you pray. Talk to Him from your heart.

The Sign Of The Cross

Catholics begin their day, their prayer, and their activities with the Sign of the Cross. The Sign of the Cross strengthens us in temptations and difficulties and reminds us of Jesus' love for us.

**In the name of the Father,
and of the Son,
and of the Holy Spirit.
Amen.**

Amen.

This is a word
that ends our prayers.
It means:
"Please do this, my Father.
I hope what I ask will take place."

I honor and thank Jesus, the Son of God,
Who came to save us all from sin.

My Jesus, Mercy!
Sacred Heart of Jesus. I trust in You.
Dear Jesus, I love you.
Dear Jesus help me to do as I am told.
Bless my father and my mother.
Bless all those I love.
Dear Jesus, You loved Your dear Mother so.
You did what she told You.
Help me to be good to my mother.
Dear Infant Jesus, never let me make You
sad by my sins.
Jesus, when I have to do hard things,
help me to do them at once.
Dear Jesus, I am so glad that You love me.
Put Your kind hands on me and bless me.
Keep me safe from harm.
Amen.

The Lord's Prayer:
The Our Father

This prayer is the most important prayer Jesus gave us. This is the most perfect prayer. It is the summary of the whole Gospel. Jesus says to me, "Ask and you will receive." I pray this prayer with my heart many times a day.

Our Father,
who art in Heaven...

God is my Father. He is everyone's Father.
He says to call Him Abba, Daddy! He made my body
and my soul.
He gave me everything good. He made me to know Him,
to love Him, and to obey Him.
He wants me to come to Him some day in Heaven.
There I shall be very happy with Him and the Saints forever.

Hallowed be Thy name...

This means I hope everyone will love my Father in Heaven. I want them all to say kind things about Him and to praise His holy Name.

I hope everyone will know Him. I hope they will all love Him as I do.

Thy Kingdom Come...

I am a little Catholic. I love Jesus. I belong to God's Kingdom. Besides being patriotic, I am also a Christian.

I wish everyone was Catholic too. They would get so many gifts from God. They would know so many things to make them happy. They would know that God loves them, too.

Thy will be done on earth
as it is in Heaven...

In Heaven everyone does God's will. That is why everyone is happy there. There are Angels and Saints in Heaven with God. On earth, lots of people are unhappy.

They do not do what God wants. They commit sin. I wish people on earth were like the happy Saints in Heaven.

Give us this day our daily bread...

My Father in Heaven gives me everything I need.
He gives me my food. He gives me my clothes. He gives me the
Sacraments of grace. So I ask Him to keep on giving me all I
need. I know He will, if I trust in Him.

And forgive us our trespasses...

Trespasses are naughty bad things. Trespasses are my sins. Sometimes I am naughty. Sometimes I do things that are not nice. These are sins. I ask God to forgive my sins, please. He promises He will, if I am truly sorry.

As we forgive those who trespass against us.

Sometimes people are not nice to me. They hurt my feelings. They do unkind things to me. But I will not be angry. I forgive them. Then God will forgive me when I do unkind things to Him.

And lead us not into temptation...

The world is full of dangers. Sometimes bad people try to harm us. They try to make us sin. The evil spirits hate us too. We ask our Father to take care of us. We say "Please don't let us fall into sin. Please don't let us run into danger."

But deliver us from evil.

The world is full of sad things, too. The devil tries to trick us to do evil. But, we do not want to sin and be sad. We want to be happy. So we ask God to take care of us.

Little children can be hurt easily. But we pray to our Father. He won't let anything hurt us.

The Holy Spirit is the third Person
of the Blessed Trinity.
He is a divine Person and He is God.
He is also our Friend.
He wants to give us His many gifts,
blessings, graces and virtues.
Jesus gave us the Holy Spirit to help us live
in His love and in truth.

Prayer To The Holy Spirit

Come Holy Spirit, fill the hearts of
Your faithful and enkindle
in them the fire of Your love.
Send forth Your Spirit and they shall be created
and You shall renew the face of the earth.
Amen.

The Glory Be

Another important prayer is this
prayer to God.
God is One divine Being in Three Persons,
and He has existed forever.
I should speak to Each Person of God
as my Friend.
In this prayer, I praise and thank the
Trinity for making the world.
I also look forward to being
with God forever in Heaven,
where I will be someday if I love Him.

**Glory be to the Father, and to the Son,
and to the Holy Spirit.
As it was in the beginning, is now,
and ever shall be, world without end.
Amen.**

Then you offer God the whole day.
When you do this, the day becomes very
important. God is happy.
He is pleased that you give Him your day.
He blesses you.
Everything you do
will make you happier in Heaven.

**O, dear Father,
I offer You my day.
Everything I do today, I will do for You;
Please accept me as Your child.
Please take my day as my gift to You.
I want to spend it as Your Son Jesus did;
I want to act like Mary Your Mother did;
I want to make others around me happy.
Help me to spend it well.
Through Christ Our Lord. Amen.**

Then I honor our dear Mother in Heaven;
Mary who is Jesus' Mother also.

The Hail Mary

Mary is my Mother in Heaven. I pray with and to Mary. She is the model of Prayer. I always welcome Mary into my Heart. She always leads me to Jesus and teaches me to obey Him. Jesus is pleased when I pray to Mary with love.

Hail, Mary! ...

This is what the Angel Gabriel said when he visited Mary: "Rejoice!" She was invited to be the Mother of God. Mary was filled with joy. She was to be the Mother of Jesus. She is my loving Mother, too.

Full of grace! ...

Mary was very beautiful. She was very good. God loved her a great deal. She was conceived without original sin and never committed any sin. She always loved God completely.

He filled her soul with beautiful gifts, with His grace; this is God's life in her soul.

The Lord is with you ...

God the Father loved Mary. She was His daughter. God the Holy Spirit loved her like His bride.

God the Son loved her too. He was sent to dwell in her in a special way, to become her Son. She became the Mother of Jesus. She gave Him to the world.

Blessed are you
among women ...

This is what Saint Elizabeth, Mary's cousin, said to her. There have been many beautiful women who lived. There have been many holy people and good people. But Mary was the greatest of them all. She believed fully in God's Word.

And blessed is the fruit of your womb, ...

The fruit of her womb is her baby. His Name is Jesus. He is the Son of God. She is His Mother. This makes Mary and her Baby very blessed.

Jesus...

This is the Holy Name of God's Son. Jesus is divine; He is God's Son. He also became man when He became Mary's Baby. She loved Him very much, and so do I. The Holy Names of Jesus and Mary are at the heart of prayer. These two names are the most powerful and simple.

Holy Mary, Mother of God ...

Mary was very good and holy. But what made her great was this: She became God's Mother. For Jesus is God. And she is the Mother of Jesus. So she became the Mother of God.

Pray for us sinners ...

When I do naughty bad things, I become a sinner. Mary is my Mother. She loves me even when I am bad. So she prays for me. She says, "Please, Jesus, my Son, forgive my child." And He does forgive me. She teaches me to trust in Jesus.

Now and at the hour of our death... Amen

Someday we shall die. If we are good and love Jesus and His Mother, Mary will pray for us. Jesus and the saints will welcome us into Heaven. How happy we shall be if in the hour of our death Jesus and Mary bring us safely to paradise to join all of our family members that have gone before us!

Then I talk to Jesus, Mary and Joseph.
This is the Holy Family.

Jesus, Mary and Joseph,
I offer you my heart and my soul.
Jesus, Mary and Joseph,
please help me when I need your help.
Jesus, Mary and Joseph,
I give you my soul to keep in peace.
Jesus, Mary and Joseph,
keep my family safe and happy.
Amen.

The Beatitudes

Blessed are the poor in Spirit,
for theirs is the Kingdom of Heaven.

Blessed are the meek,
for they shall possess the earth.

Blessed are they who mourn,
for they shall be comforted.

Blessed are they who hunger
and thirst for justice,
for they shall be satisfied.

Blessed are the merciful,
for they shall obtain mercy.

Blessed are the pure of heart,
for they shall see God.

37

Blessed are the peacemakers,
for they shall be called children of God.

Blessed are they who suffer
persecution for justice sake,
for theirs is the Kingdom of Heaven.

The Angelus

Angelus is the Latin word that means angel.
The Angel of the Lord declared unto Mary,
and she conceived of the Holy Spirit.

Hail Mary...

Mary answered the Angel
in these lovely words.
Behold the handmaid of the Lord.
Be it done unto me according to Your word.

Hail Mary...

Then the Son of God came to earth
near the heart of Mary.
And the Word was made Flesh,
and lived among us.

Hail Mary...

We ask our Mother to take care of us.

Pray for us
O Holy Mother of God,
that we may become worthy
of the promises of Christ.

Then we all pray together.

Lord, fill our hearts with Your grace; once, through the message of an angel You revealed to us the incarnation of Your Son; now, through His suffering and death lead us to the glory of His resurrection. We ask this through Christ our Lord. Amen.

The Apostles' Creed - What We Believe

On Sundays and Holy Days, we pray the Creed.
This is a great Act of Faith. It was written a long time ago.
It shows that we know the truth. It says that we have listened
to Jesus Christ. It means that we believe in His Church.

I believe ... This is our great act
of faith. Jesus came to teach us about
God and how to reach Heaven.
He loved us and wanted us
to live forever.
So what He taught us was taught to
us by our best friend.
He was also the wisest of men and
the divine Son of God.
He said to His Apostles,
"Go out and teach all nations."
And, "He that hears you, hears me."
So I believe Jesus. And I believe
the Apostles, whom He sent.

STS. PETER & PAUL

I believe in God ...
I believe that He is my dear
and Heavenly Father.
Long, long ago He created the earth.
He has all power; He used that
power to make the world.
He set the sun, the stars,
and the moon in the sky.
He filled the land with good
and beautiful things.
And then He made for me
a lovely mansion in Heaven.
If I am good on earth, I shall be
happy in Heaven.

I believe ... in Jesus Christ,
His only Son, Our Lord ...

The Second Person of the Blessed
Trinity came to earth.
He was conceived by the Holy Spirit.
Mary was His lovely Mother.
Because He was born in Bethlehem,
we have Christmas Day.
He taught us all truth;
He did nothing but good for all.
He said, "I am the way and the truth,
and the life."

He suffered under Pontius Pilate ...
He is my Savior, my Master, my Lord,
and my God.
I believe that He suffered
and died for me.
How good and generous Jesus was!
He took upon Himself the sins
of all the world, my sins too.
He was condemned by
the Roman governor, Pontius Pilate.

He was crucified died
and was buried ...
He died on the Cross for my sins
and the sins of all mankind.
He suffered the Passion so that we
could be forgiven by God.
And when He died,
He went down into limbo
and freed the souls
imprisoned there.

He rose from the dead ...

What a wonderful day Easter is!
I believe that on that happy day
Jesus rose from the dead.
Never again would He die;
never again would He suffer.
And because He rose,
I shall rise someday. I shall live forever.
Then on Ascension Thursday,
He went up into Heaven.
He sits upon a beautiful Throne,
asking mercy and grace for us.
And when we die, He will come to judge us.
If we are good, we shall enter
into eternal happiness with Him.

I believe in the Holy Spirit ...
This is the Third Person of the
Blessed Trinity.
Jesus promised that He would come
and be our friend.
He would teach us all truth.
He would light our ways.
He would be our strength
and give us grace.
So He came to the Apostles
on the feast of Pentecost.
He comes to me in Confirmation.

I believe in the holy
Catholic Church...
I believe all that it teaches.
It is the Church of Jesus Christ.
It is the Church of the Apostles.
So I believe that it exists on earth,
in Heaven, and in purgatory.
I believe that my sins
can be forgiven if I'm sorry.
I believe that if I am good
I shall live forever.
Amen.

Then you ask your Guardian Angel
to take care of you.
When you were born,
God gave you an Angel for a friend.
He is always with you.
He protects you from harm.
He watches over you when you sleep.
He is a dear friend.
He likes you to talk to him.

**O, Angel of God,
my Guardian dear
to whom God's love
commits me here,
ever this day,
be at my side,
to light, to guard,
to rule and guide.
Amen.**

What happens when you pray?
Well, God listens and smiles and says,
"I'll take care of you, My child."
Maybe you can't hear Him.
That isn't necessary.
Right away, He is near you.
He helps you to be good.
He drives away evil things
and evil people who might hurt you.
He says, "My child is good, and loves Me;
I will make him/her happy."
When you ask for things that are good for you,
He gives them to you.
He helps you grow to be a strong child.
He brings you safely through life,
so you will grow up to be
good Catholic adults.

"Let the little children come to me, ..."
Mark 10:14